Arthur Mascarenhas
Rodrigo Alves

A general approach to the reinsurance market in Brazil

Arthur Mascarenhas
Rodrigo Alves

A general approach to the reinsurance market in Brazil

Final Project of Course Conclusion - Department of Statistical Methods, Institute of Mathematics, UFRJ

ScienciaScripts

Imprint

Any brand names and product names mentioned in this book are subject to trademark, brand or patent protection and are trademarks or registered trademarks of their respective holders. The use of brand names, product names, common names, trade names, product descriptions etc. even without a particular marking in this work is in no way to be construed to mean that such names may be regarded as unrestricted in respect of trademark and brand protection legislation and could thus be used by anyone.

Cover image: www.ingimage.com

This book is a translation from the original published under ISBN 978-620-2-17520-3.

Publisher:
Sciencia Scripts
is a trademark of
Dodo Books Indian Ocean Ltd. and OmniScriptum S.R.L publishing group

120 High Road, East Finchley, London, N2 9ED, United Kingdom
Str. Armeneasca 28/1, office 1, Chisinau MD-2012, Republic of Moldova, Europe
Printed at: see last page
ISBN: 978-620-5-94764-7

DEDICATION

This work is dedicated to our families and friends who gave us the necessary support for the elaboration and conclusion of this course work.

THANKS

We thank the teachers and students of the Institute who have contributed to our training and development.

We also thank our families who gave us all the necessary support:

Paulo Cesar Matos Mascarenhas, Angela Alves Julião, Cesar Julião Mascarenhas, Raianna Pacheco Almeida Pamphiro, Jurandy Mascarenhas, Gracília Matos Mascarenhas.

Oswaldo Meirelles Alves Neto, Eneida de Figueiredo Barreto Alves and Felipe Barreto Alves.

SUMMARY

MASCARENHAS, Arthur Julião; ALVES, Rodrigo Barreto. Analysis of the Reinsurance Market in Brazil with Some Practical Applications. Rio de Janeiro, XXXXX, 2013. Projeto Final de Conclusão de Curso, Departamento de Métodos Estatísticos, Instituto de Matemática, Universidade Federal do Rio de Janeiro, Rio de Janeiro, December 2013.

The main objective of this paper is to explore the opening of the reinsurance market in Brazil, its peculiarities and importance. In order to contribute to a better understanding of this process, we highlight the main technical foundations of reinsurance, the importance of its use for solvency and stabilization of results of insurance companies and the evolution of the opening of the market, as well as its current composition. The technical foundations of reinsurance were explained concisely in order to improve understanding for the application of the theory concerning the process of breaking the monopoly of the Brazilian reinsurance market.

Keywords: Reinsurance, market opening, monopoly, IRB

SUMMARY

CHAPTER 1

INTRODUCTION

In Brazil, the history of reinsurance is directly related to the history of insurance, which has undergone several phases of evolution and learning over time.

The Brazilian government tried to implement measures to try to reduce the flow of capital abroad, but due to resistance from the foreign companies themselves, none of the measures adopted were successful. With the creation of the Brazilian Reinsurance Institute (IRB), which implemented new instruments so that the Brazilian insurance and reinsurance market could evolve, the problem of transferring premiums abroad was alleviated and domestic companies were strengthened, and began to compete with foreign companies on a more equal footing, since the IRB determined the insurance rates and these were equal for all companies operating at the time.

Before the creation of the IRB, insurance and reinsurance premiums were exported from the country and domestic insurance companies could not compete with foreign insurance companies.

"Until 1939, the year of creation of the Instituto de Resseguro do Brasil - IRB, what we saw was a complete anarchy of rates combined with an inferiority of the Brazilian companies compared to their foreign counterparts. (ALVIM, 1996, p. 327).

In December 1999, the National Congress approved the Law n[5] 9.932 of 20 December 1999, breaking the monopoly for reinsurance activity in Brazil, until then delegated solely and exclusively to the IRB. A year later the IRB was transformed into IRB-Brasil Resseguros S.A., in the form of a public limited company with closed capital and mixed economy, maintaining all the ordinary shares, with voting rights, in the power of the Union.

Despite the approval of Law n° 9.932 of 1999, the privatization of the institute of Reinsurance Brazil did not occur, because the Workers' Party (PT) filed a Direct Action of Unconstitutionality - Adin n° 2. 223-7 contesting precepts of the aforementioned Law and the acting president of the Federal Supreme Court at the time Minister Marco Aurélio Farias

Mello granted the injunction pleaded by Adin n 2.223-7 challenging precepts of the cited Law and the acting president of the Federal Supreme Court at the time, Minister Marco Aurélio de Farias Mello, granted the injunction sought by Adin n° 2.223-7 and suspended the effectiveness of Law n° 9.932/99.

The breaking of the reinsurance monopoly only occurred in fact and law after the publication of Supplementary Law 126 of 2007 and later Resolution no.° 168 of the National Council of Private Insurance (CNSP) of 2007, which opened the reinsurance market in Brazil and defined the parameters and restrictions for the establishment of other national or foreign reinsurers in the country.

In December 2010, three years after the opening of the reinsurance market, CNSP, in order to protect the Brazilian market and contain the export of reinsurance premium from the country, published CNSP Resolutions n° 224 and 225, determining that local insurance and reinsurance companies may not transfer their liabilities assumed in insurance reinsurance and retrocession in Brazil to companies linked or belonging to the same financial conglomerate based abroad and that local insurers must necessarily contract with local reinsurers at least 40% of each reinsurance cession.

In March 2011, the CNSP published CNSP Resolution n° 232, which revoked CNSP Resolution n° 224 and determined that local insurance and reinsurance companies may transfer up to a maximum of 20% of the liabilities assumed in insurance, reinsurance and retrocession in Brazil to companies linked to or belonging to the same financial conglomerate based abroad.

With the opening of the reinsurance market in Brazil and the loss of the IRB monopoly, it is expected to promote (a) increased competitiveness in the sector, (b) reduction in reinsurance rates and, consequently, insurance rates, (c) stimulus to the adoption of new technologies and the development of new products and, finally, (d) development of the insurance market.

CHAPTER 2

REINSURANCE FUNDAMENTALS

2.1   *Definition*

The Superintendence of Private Insurance (Susep), through Resolution CNSP n[5] 168 of 2007, which provides for the activity of reinsurance, retrocession and its intermediation, chapter III, Art. 2^5 , considers the following definitions:

I - Ceding: The insurance company that contracts the reinsurance operation or the reinsurer that contracts the retrocession operation;

VIII - Reinsurance: Transfer of risks from a ceding company, for its own protection, to one or more reinsurers, through automatic or facultative contracts; and

IX   - Retrocession: Transfer of reinsurance risks from reinsurers, for their own protection, to reinsurers or local insurance companies, through automatic or facultative contracts.

Basically, reinsurance is the transfer of insurance risk from one insurer to another through a contract in which one of the insurers (the reinsurer) agrees, in exchange for a reinsurance premium, to indemnify the other (the ceding insurer) from part or all of the financial consequences of certain loss exposures covered by one or more of the ceding insurer's insurance policies. Reinsurance is commonly known as "insurers' insurance".

The ceding insurer may be referred to as the direct insurer, the reinsured, or simply the cedant. An insurance company may have reinsurance transactions where it is the ceding insurer and others where it is the reinsurer.

Normally, the reinsurer does not assume the entire insurance risk of the ceding insurer. The reinsurance contract usually requires the ceding insurer to retain part of its original liability.

In general, the reinsurance operation has as its main objective to protect the cedant from the risk assumed by it, pulverizing it, through specific contracts. This operation causes the reinsurer to assume this risk, for remuneration, and to agree to indemnify the cedant in relation to the loss incurred, in accordance with the assumptions established in the reinsurance contract.

According to CNSP Resolution n° 168, of 2007, reinsurers may transfer part of the liability that was accepted in reinsurance contracts to other reinsurers. This type of action is characterized as another contract, and is called a retrocession contract.

When risk retrocession occurs, a reinsurer (retroceding) transfers part or all of the risk that was assumed in the reinsurance contract to another reinsurer or to an insurer (retrocessionary).

We then realize that retrocession is similar to reinsurance, since it also involves risk spreading. However, reinsurance and retrocession operations differ in relation to the parties involved in each operation.

Figure 1: Reinsurance flow, from insured to reinsurer.
Source: own

2.2. *The need for reinsurance*

Reinsurance allows the insurer to limit its exposure and reduce the volatility of its results, keeping its business more stable over the years.

Another relevant factor consists in the fact of a catastrophe occurrence, whether natural or man-made, where the reinsurance will support the cedant in the indemnities of claims to the insured.

Reinsurance is a mechanism that insurers use to protect themselves from the financial consequences of the insurance cover they provide to their clients.

With risk dilution, the insurer will be able to capture more risks in the market and increasingly increase its portfolio of insureds, preserving its stable results.

2.3. *Reinsurance Functions*

Reinsurance has several functions for insurers, five of which are highlighted below. An insurer may use several different reinsurance contracts to benefit from these functions;

i.   Increase the capacity to assume large risks;

ii.   Protect against catastrophes;

iii. Stabilise the accident rate;

iv.   Facilitating exit from a market segment;

v.   To provide assistance in underwriting risks.

2.3.1. Increase the capacity to assume large risks

One function of reinsurance is to increase the cedant's capacity to assume large risks. The maximum amount of the retained sum insured or the limit of liability is also called the retention limit.

This function provides ample capacity for the cedant to underwrite a high coverage limit for a single risk and produce a high annual volume of premium issued.

"The increase in portfolio capacity gives the power to the insurer to accept risks in excess of its acceptance limit, usually, stipulated by insurance authority of each country." (Gropello 1997, p. 35):

Reinsurers provide insurers with a capacity to assume large risks by accepting exposures to claims that they are unwilling or unable to retain. This function allows insurers whose ability to underwrite large risks is limited to participate in a broader market. For example, an insurer may wish to compete in home insurance markets where the value of homes exceeds the amount it is willing to safely retain. Reinsurance allows the insurer to increase its market share while limiting the financial consequences of potential claims.

2.3.2. Protecting against disasters

Catastrophe reinsurance is designed to support multiple losses, from several policies underwritten by the insurer, arising from a single catastrophic event.

Through catastrophe reinsurance the insurer limits its losses to a predetermined amount, as per conditions agreed in reinsurance contracts, and protects itself from a large financial loss.

The pricing of this type of reinsurance contract is quite specific and requires a geographical detail in the information provided by the cedant.

Potentially catastrophic events are fire, windstorms, earthquakes, industrial explosions, aircraft disasters; and can result in significant liability claims and property damage. Unless appropriate reinsurance coverage is in place, catastrophes can greatly reduce the bottom line or even threaten the solvency of an insurer.

2.3.3. Stabilising the accident rate

Through reinsurance cedants are able to offset the effects of fluctuating claims ratios, due to demographic, economic, social, natural forces or by simple chance, which occur from one year to the next, and may be applied to one type of insurance (such as life insurance), one modality (such as group life), or all the insurances operated by an insurer.

A volatile claim rate can affect the insurer in various aspects such as:

Value of shares traded on stock exchanges;

Classification of the financial situation, carried out by independent rating agencies;

Changes in the risk underwriting, claims and marketing departments.

Shake the confidence of the sales area;

Lead to insolvency.

Stabilising loss ratios is an important function of reinsurance because it helps financial planning and supports the insurer's growth, stimulating capital investment and stable financial results.

2.3.4. Facilitating exit from a market segment

A market segment can be a class of business, a geographical area or a type of insurance. Reinsurance can help an insurer withdraw from a certain segment because it is no longer profitable, is undesirable or does not apply to its strategic plan.

There are a few options to exit a market segment, among them there are three main ones:

i. Mechanism known as "run-off": Stop selling new insurance policies and keep insurance in force until all policies expire;
ii. If regulations allow, cancel all policies and return unearned premium to policyholders;
iii. Exit the market segment through reinsurance which is known as portfolio reinsurance.

In the latter option, the reinsurer covers the claims exposures of all policies of a type of insurance, class or geographic area. These groupings are called portfolios.

With portfolio transfer, the risk is fully covered by reinsurance. This operation becomes even more expensive when the portfolio is not profitable.

For technical or commercial reasons, an insurer that no longer wishes to operate in a particular line of business or geographical area can use reinsurance to continue to meet its obligations to policyholders, brokers and authorities.

2.3.5 To provide assistance in underwriting risks

As the reinsurer normally does business with a large number of insurers, it accumulates knowledge about methods of rating, risk inspection, complex claims, determining deductibles appropriate for each activity and adjusting coverage for products.

Thus, it develops expertise in risk prevention, claims regulation and guidance in the adoption of new insurance products, helping insurers with little experience to operate in new markets.

2.4 Retention Limit

2.4.1 Significance

The retention limit is the maximum sum insured or the limit of liability that an insurer has established it can assume on a risk.

Susep, through CNSP Resolution n[5] 276, of 2013, established rules for the calculation of the retention limit of insurers and reinsurers, in which the limits should be at most equal to 5% of the adjusted net assets and, for limits higher than this, prior authorization from Susep becomes necessary. Therefore, CNSP Resolution n[5] 40 of 2000, which defined that the retention limit should be between 0.3% and 3% of the adjusted net assets, was revoked.

2.4.2. Critical factors in determining the Retention Limit

The retention limit is determined as a function of the insurer's net assets and risk appetite and is influenced by the following factors:

Limit of cover, types and cost of reinsurance available;

Specific characteristics of a claims exposure;

The amount of a claim or set of claims that can be borne by the insurer without adversely affecting its profitability or its equity;

Maximum amount of the sum insured or the liability limit per risk allowed by Susep.

In either case, the retention is ultimately the maximum amount that the insurer, based on its financial situation, is prepared to assume in a claim, without this implying a relevant fluctuation of its results.

Logically, the higher the retention, the greater the possibility of fluctuation in an insurer's results.

2.5. *Subscribe*

Risk underwriting is the process that involves making a selective decision on acceptable risks, determining the premium to be charged, the conditions and terms of the contract and all specific negotiation on each risk, of each branch.

The main objective of underwriting is to offer the appropriate coverage for each type of risk, as well as the appropriate conditions and prices. The responsibility for underwriting the risk lies with the portfolio underwriter.

In the case of automatic reinsurance, the insurer underwrites the risk and cedes the applicable reinsurance premium to the reinsurer, with no need for risk-by-risk consultation.

In the case of facultative reinsurance, normally, the insurer underwrites the risk and offers it to the reinsurer, who may accept it or not, depending on the conditions offered. However, there are also cases in which the insurer presents the risk and the conditions to the reinsurer, which evaluates and prices it. It is up to the insurer to accept or not this price.

2.6. *Coinsurance*

Co-insurance consists of an operation carried out by two or more insurers, with the aim of covering the same risk. Thus, one realises the possibility of large risks being covered by insurers with lower retention limits. Therefore, each insurer assumes responsibility for a part of the amount.

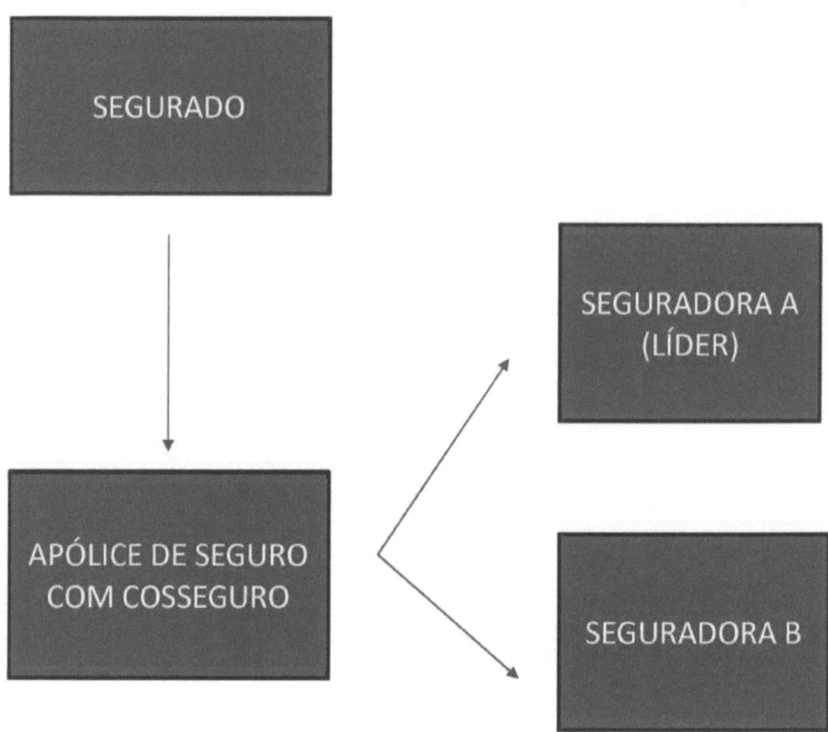

Figure 2: Flow of coinsurance.

Source: Own

The policy is issued by the leading insurer, the one with whom the insured made the quotation, and in it is established the participation of each insurer in the total sum insured. This participation determines the proportional division of the premium paid by the insured among the insurers.

Supep, through SUSEP Circular nº 287, of 2005, which provides for the registration of policies, endorsements issued and coinsurance accepted by the companies

insurers in their own accounts with registration, custody and financial settlement institutions, considers that:

"Art. 3- Issued endorsements and accepted coinsurance shall contain the registration number in the institution of registration, custody and financial liguidation, being the same

considered as an element of characterization of the contract."

Sole Paragraph. The deadline for issuing the endorsement shall be 2 (two) business days, counted from the date of acceptance of the proposal.

Art. 6º The data to be submitted to the registration, custody and financial settlement institutions by the insurance companies, with the aim of granting the registration number in the registration, custody and financial settlement institution, must comply with the specifications contained in the appendices to this Circular.

§ 1º After receiving this data, the insurance company shall obtain the policy number from the institution, which, obligatorily, shall be followed, taking into consideration its composition:

I. Susep registration code of the insurance company;

II. Year of issue of the policy or endorsement;

III. Code of the branch of operation at Susep;

IV. Sequential number per trade branch generated exclusively by the registration, custody and financial settlement institution.

§ Paragraph 2 The provisions of Paragraph 1 of this Article shall apply to the acceptance of coinsurance.

CHAPTER 3

Types of Reinsurance

Reinsurance can be divided into two types: automatic, better known as a reinsurance contract, and facultative.

3.1   Automatic Reinsurance

Known as obligatory reinsurance or a reinsurance contract, automatic reinsurance covers an entire class or portfolio of risks. It guarantees that each risk that falls within the contract description will be automatically reinsured.

It should be noted that the reinsurer agrees in advance to reinsure all risks that fit the description made in the contract. With automatic reinsurance, insurers have their main needs met.

Generally, automatic reinsurance contracts are structured to meet the needs of an insurer to reinsure many risks over a period of time. Although this period, most often, is one year, the relationship between the cedant and the reinsurer usually extends for much longer, through term endorsements, contract renewals and new products.

With this, there may be anti-selection, as reinsurers are obliged to accept ceded risks. Antiselection occurs when the cedant decides to reinsure only the risks that have a high probability of suffering claims, because the retention of these claims is undesirable for the insurer. In order to avoid anti-selection in automatic contracts, reinsurers usually seek information on the integrity and experience of the insurer's management and the degree to which its publicly announced underwriting guidelines are followed in practice.

3.2   Facultative Reinsurance

In facultative reinsurance, the insurer negotiates a separate reinsurance contract for each risk it wishes to reinsure and the reinsurer analyses whether or not to accept the risk offered.

There is no obligation on the insurer to purchase reinsurance, nor is there any obligation on the reinsurer to provide reinsurance. Often this is a form of commercial approximation between the two parties.

The facultative contract has a fixed term and cannot be cancelled by either party, unless some contractual obligation is not fulfilled, such as, for example, non-payment of the reinsurance premium.

Facultative reinsurance has the following four functions:

i.   To provide capacity to the cedant to accept risks whose value exceeds the limit of cover of its automatic reinsurance contracts;

ii. Reduce the cedant's exposure in a particular location or geographical area. For example, a marine risk underwriter may be considering accepting several marine transport insurances whose cargoes, from different insureds, will be in the same warehouse. The underwriter may use facultative reinsurance for some of these risks, thereby reducing the insurer's total exposure in that location;

iii. Cover a risk with atypical characteristics, maintaining the favourable claim experience of the automatic reinsurance contract. Maintaining the favourable experience of automatic reinsurance contracts is important because the reinsurer sets the conditions and price of its coverage based on certain expectations. The inclusion of a risk that is incompatible with the typical risks that comprise the ceding party's portfolio may excessively increase the claim rate and lead to the termination of the contract or an increase in its price;

iv. Covering risks of certain classes that are excluded from automatic reinsurance contracts.

Facultative reinsurance cover is normally more expensive compared to automatic reinsurance because it tends to have a higher probability of claims and its administrative costs are usually high.

The characteristics of facultative reinsurance are:

Oldest form of reinsurance;

No obligation to accept or cede;

Flexibility;

Anti-selection against the reinsurer;

High administrative cost;

Policy cannot be issued before cover is paid up;

3.3 Types of reinsurance contracts

As previously stated, reinsurance contracts are negotiated between the cedant and the reinsurer. Each contract negotiated is unique and its terms reflect the needs of the insurer and the availability of reinsurers in the market that meet those needs.

The insurer may use several types of contract that together form a reinsurance programme.

Reinsurance contracts may be proportional or non-proportional, as shown in the table below:

Figure 3: Types of reinsurance contract

Proportional	Non-proportional
Proportional share of the premium issued	Reinsurance premium calculated separately
Proportional participation in sinsitro	Participation in the claim in excess of one priority

Source: Own

3.3.1 Proportional Share Reinsurance

In proportional reinsurance the insurer and the reinsurer always participate with the same percentage in the risk. Reinsurer and cedant establish a fixed percentage for the cession by the cedant and the acceptance by the reinsurer of the risks and respective premiums and claims (including claims adjustment and settlement expenses).

For example, out of a reinsurer's 30% stake in a risk and a cedant's 70% retention, premiums and claims are split in proportion to the respective liabilities.

Example:

Quota Share: 30%.

Capacity: BRL 100,000,000.00

Policy A:

IS: R$ 80,000,000.00

Prize: R$ 20.000,00

Figure 4: Example of proportional share reinsurance.

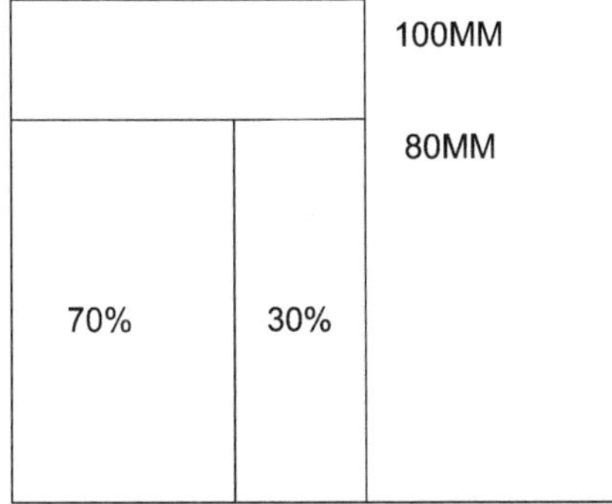

IS Seguradora: R$ 56,000,000.00 (70%)

IS Reinsurer: R$ 24.000.000,00   (30%)

Insurance Premium: R$ 14.000,00 (70%)

Reinsurance Premium: R$ 6.000,00 (30%)

It should be noted that risks that have a small reinsured amount will also be reinsured respecting the percentage established in the contract.

The following are some disadvantages and advantages of share insurance for the insurer:

Disadvantages:

- High cost of reinsurance - As the cedant cannot vary its retention on a specific risk, it ends up ceding premiums relating to small risks. Risks, which it could fully assume;

- Heterogeneity of the portfolio - The risks retained are not homogeneous, since the grantor retains a fixed percentage of all the risks subscribed, whose insured values are varied, not giving equilibrium to the portfolio;
- It does not adequately protect against high (individual) claims;

- It does not adequately protect against the build-up of risk within an event;

Advantages:

- Easy administration and operation, as the same percentage of reinsurance is applied to premiums and claims;
- Boost equity;
- Increase the capacity to take big risks;
- Increase risk spreading.

3.3.2. Proportional Excess of Liability Reinsurance

Excess liability is a proportional reinsurance that covers risks whose insured importance exceeds a stipulated value, called the insurer's full. When the insured importance exceeds the full, the reinsurer assumes the excess value, i.e. the difference between the insured importance and the retention imite (L.R. or L.T.).

"This is a proportional contract like the quota share, because when the insured importance (I.S.) exceeds the L.T., the insurer transfers the surplus proportionally. From that moment on we have a proportional contract and whatever the amount of the claim, the insurer recovers the proportion transferred". (Paulo Pereira Ferreira, 2002).

IS $\leq$ LT $\rightarrow$ No reinsurance.

IS > LT $\rightarrow$ Insurer cedes proportionately.

Example:

Retention: R$ 20,000,000.00

Capacity: BRL 100,000,000.00

Policy A:

IS: R$ 80,000,000.00

Prize: R$ 20.000,00

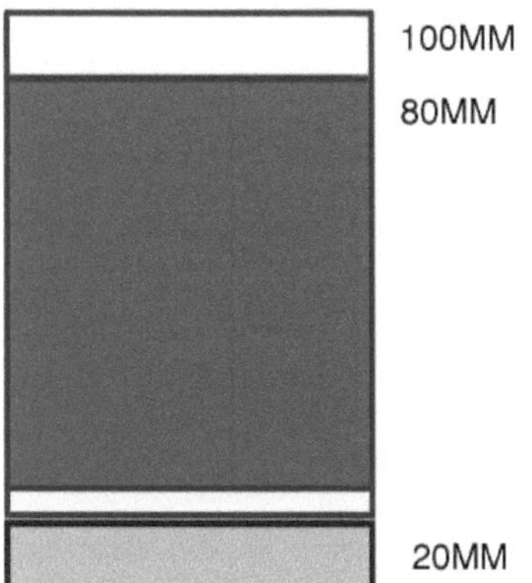

Figure 5: Example 1 of proportional excess of liability reinsurance

Policy B:
IS: R$ 10,000,000
Prize: R$ 2.000,00

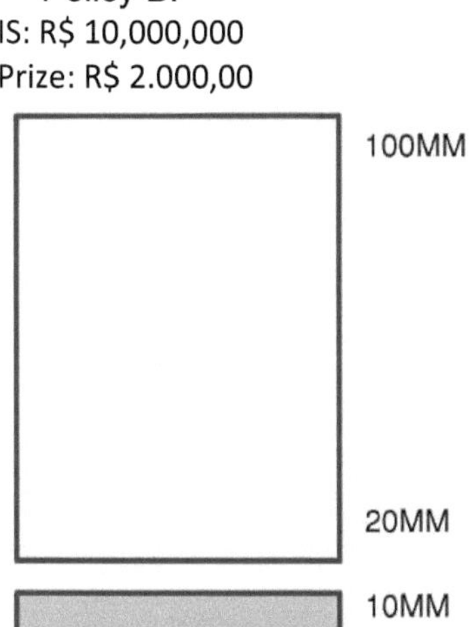

Figure 6: Example 2 of proportional excess of liability reinsurance.

IS Insurance Company: R$ 10,000,000.00 (100%)
IS Reinsurer: R$ 0.00 (0%)
Insurance Premium: R$ 2.000,00 (100%)
Reinsurance Premium: R$ 0.00 (0%)

IS Insurance Company: R$ 20,000,000.00 (25%)

IS Reinsurer: R$ 60,000,000.00 (75%)

Insurance Premium: R$ 5.000,00 (25%)

Reinsurance Premium: R$ 15.000,00 (75%)

Excess of liability constitutes a type of proportional reinsurance where the percentage participation of the insurer and the reinsurer is variable according to the risk. Some observations should be highlighted about this type of reinsurance, such as, in cases where the claim is smaller than the LT, but there was an assignment, there will still be

a proportional recovery; the non-coverage of risks whose insured amount is less than the retention limit of the insurer and the cost of administration being greater than the reinsurance share. This cost is higher because insurers need to keep a record of the cessions and periodically provide the reinsurer with a report, called a borderô, which must contain all the risks ceded to the contract.

It is common to use both types of proportional reinsurance in the same contract. When the quota share "cannot absorb by itself the entire portfolio, it is possible to complete it with the contract by excess of liability" (Swiss Re, 1997, p.71).

Moreover, "with proportional protection, it is known that when an assignment is made, a portion of any and all claims will always be borne by the reinsurer" (Germaine, 1985, p. 68).

Below are some advantages and disadvantages of this type of proportional reinsurance contract:

Disadvantages:

- Operational complexity;
- Higher cost of administration; and
- Does not protect the portfolio against risk accumulation within an event. Advantages:
- Better balance of the insurer's portfolio;
- There is no passing of risk within the insurer's retention; and
- Adequate protection against high (individual) claims.

3.3.3.Non-Proportional Excess of Loss reinsurance

Type of reinsurance where a loss limit is fixed for the insurer on one or more isolated risks. This loss limit is called priority. Excess damage guarantees recovery under the amount of indemnity and expenses exceeding that limit. "The basis of the formulation of the excess damage plan is the behaviour of the reinsured's portfolio in recent years, that is, the frequency distribution of indemnities and expenses paid". (Nascentes, 1996, p. 15).

There are basically three types of excess of loss reinsurance, also called non-proportional reinsurance. Each one has specific characteristics and purposes, excess of loss reinsurance by risk, excess of loss by event/catastrophe and aggregate excess of loss (stop loss).

The excess of loss reinsurance premium is negotiated based on the probability of the amounts of claims exceeding the priority that was established, that is, the reinsurer receives a portion of the premiums that is not proportional in relation to the ceded liability. The cedant's limit, on the other hand, is set at a level that covers the ranges of claim values that occur most assiduously.

In certain excess of loss contracts we find a coparticipation clause, which requires the insurer to retain a specified percentage of the losses above its priority. The purpose of this clause is to create an incentive for the insurer to efficiently manage the risks exceeding its limit.

Claims adjustment and settlement expenses can be incurred in two ways:

Proportional distribution of expenses between insurer and reinsurer based on each party's share of the claim: If the value of the claim does not exceed the priority, the insurer is responsible for all expenses of claims adjustment and settlement.

Addition of claim adjustment and settlement expenses to the value of the claim: The reinsurer may pay a claim whose value, without adding expenses, would not exceed the priority.

It should be noted that in this type of reinsurance contract there may be reintegration of coverage, where insurer and reinsurer negotiate the amount and cost before the contract begins to run. This reintegration is triggered in the event of claims that reach the contract limit. The number of reinstatements may be limited or unlimited, with or without payment of additional premium.

3.3.3.I. Pricing of Non-Proportional contracts

In the pricing of non-proportional contracts, reinsurance rates have no direct relationship with insurance rates. The cost of reinsurance is negotiated through a rate applicable on the insurance premium of the protected portfolio.

The focus of non-proportional reinsurance pricing is on claims that exceed the priority and limit of the reinsurance contract.

The following figure demonstrates how excess damage cover works, assuming that the insurer's priority is $5 and the reinsurer's priority is $10, so that every claim that exceeds $15, the excess is paid by the insurer:

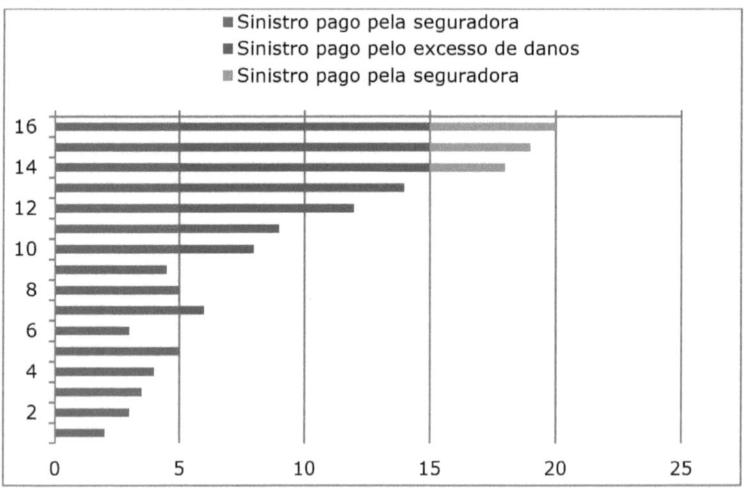

Figure 7: Illustrative table of excess damage cover.

Source: Adapted from FUNENSEG's presentation of the principles of reinsurance.

The premiums that the reinsurer charges for assuming risks must be sufficient to pay claims, cover costs related to its business activity and make a profit.

"The technical premium is the portion of the premium necessary for the payment of expected claims. On the other hand, we have the security load, intended to cover possible fluctuations. It serves to indemnify the investor for the risk contracted" (Bidino, 2009).

Premiums cannot be established with absolute precision, so there must be a margin of safety.

The amount of information provided by the insurer tends to be inversely proportional to the price of the reinsurance cover, because the pricing will be more precise and the degree of uncertainty will be lower. Basically, the reinsurer will have more credibility in the insurer's data, so it can use the actual standards. If there is not enough information, there will be estimates that will be more conservative, increasing the price of reinsurance.

Unlike proportional reinsurance, in which for pricing, basically only information on cession, total annual premiums, costs and claims is required; for pricing non-proportional covers, detailed information on individual claims is required. Thus one can project the future annual claim rate of the reinsurance cover.

The objective of pricing is to estimate as accurately as possible the claims distribution valid for the contract year. Once this distribution has been determined, the technical premium and the safety margin can be deducted, thus arriving at the price of the non-proportional cover.

The information required for pricing a non-proportional contract is:

Priority and limit of the contract;

Estimated premium for the duration of the contract;

Amounts insured broken down by bands;

Number of policies corresponding to each band;

Premium issued net of brokerage corresponding to each band;

Number of claims corresponding to each band;

IS, number of policies, premiums and claims for at least the last 3 years;

Triangulation of claims; and

List of the largest claims of at least 3 years.

Pricing is done based on two methods, experience and exposure. The use of these methods and adjustments to the prices is largely in the hands and judgement of the underwriters, as their experience in relation to the particularities of the market, the insurer and the portfolio will be reflected in the price calculation.

The experience method considers the claims occurred in the past, adjusting them so as to offer an idea of the claims load to be considered in the future. To establish the price, in addition to monetary correction, possible portfolio growth and changes in the underwriting policy of the insurer must be considered, among other factors. The greatest difficulty in pricing consists in the fact that the retrospection of previous experiences must be made in the most distant past possible in order to have sufficient statistical basis, but only the most recent years allow valid conclusions for the current portfolio.

The exposure method draws on the insurer's current portfolio which is combined with the claims experience of the market. For this pricing method, the total technical premium and claims distribution are required, i.e. number of risks, average IS, original insurance rate and claims ratio.

Instead of claims distributions, so-called exposure curves are used in practice. The curve shows how the technical premium, depending on the priority, should be shared between insurer and reinsurer based on market experience. Thus, for each set of risks the technical premium per non-proportional band can be defined.

3.3.3.2. Excess of Risk Damage

O excess of loss per risk limits the insurer's loss per individual claim. The reinsurer is responsible for the excess portion of the priority. As stated earlier, excess damage can be divided into several bands.

Advantages:
- More efficient way of stabilising the claim rate;
- Easy administration; and

- Lower administrative costs.

Disadvantages:

- It does not "relieve" the pressure on equity;
- All claims below priority are the responsibility of the insurer.

Example:

Priority: R$ 2,000,000.00
Capacity: R$ 50,000,000.00
P band: 3MM xs 2MM
2^band:10MMxs5MM
3- range: 10MM xs 15MM
4- range: 25MM xs 25MM

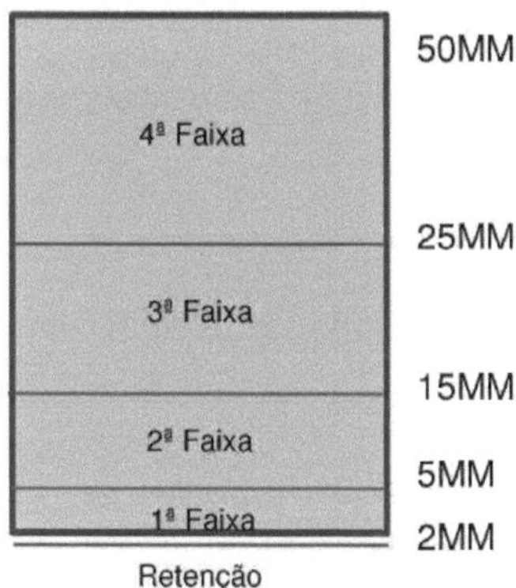

Figure 8: Example of non-proportional excess of loss reinsurance

3.3.3.3. Event/Catastrophe Damage Excess

Excess damage per event/catastrophe limits the insured's loss with respect to several claims that arise from the same event or a series of events with the same casual nexus. As with excess of damages per risk, the reinsurer is liable for the excess portion of the established priority.

These events are usually catastrophic like tornadoes, hurricanes and earthquakes that can cause billions of dollars in damage.

Advantages:

- Disaster protection;
- Accumulation of risk in a single event; and

- It allows the insurer to retain a larger portion of its gross premium.

Disadvantages:

- It does not relieve the insurer of its responsibility to maintain the unearned premium reserve relating to policies covered by reinsurance.

3.3.3.4. Excess of Aggregate Damage - Stop Loss

Aggregate excess of loss is the type of reinsurance that limits the annual loss ratio (percentage ratio between premium income and claims payments) of the insurer, based on a predetermined index. Also known as stop loss, it is a modality in which the insurer guarantees ample coverage against annual variations in the loss ratio in a line of business or in the insurer's entire portfolio. In this model, priority is established by a percentage of the loss ratio.

Advantages:

- It meets the need of portfolios where the volume of small individual claims can absorb a large part of the premium revenue, as in the health business.
- Recommended for portfolios in which the claim/premium ratios vary greatly.

Disadvantages:

- Expensive compared to other types of reinsurance.
- The reinsurer only makes the recovery payment after the end of the contract.

3.3.4 Term of Reinsurance Contracts

Reinsurance contracts are usually valid for a period of twelve months. However, there are also contracts of unlimited duration that are only terminated by cancellation requested by either party. It is assumed that the duration is annual, but if neither party expresses a desire to cancel within the prescribed period, the contract continues.

3.3.4.I. Risk Attaching Basis - Initiated Risks

This criterion is based on the beginning of validity of the risks that will be assumed by the insurer, that is, all policies whose risks are initiated within the period of validity of the reinsurance contract will be guaranteed.

"The reinsurance contract that adopts this criterion only expires when all the policies that have commenced in its term expire. In some cases, a time limit is included after the contract expires." (Fontana, 2009, p.24)

The figure below exemplifies the coverage criteria for reinsurance contracts using the risk attaching term base.

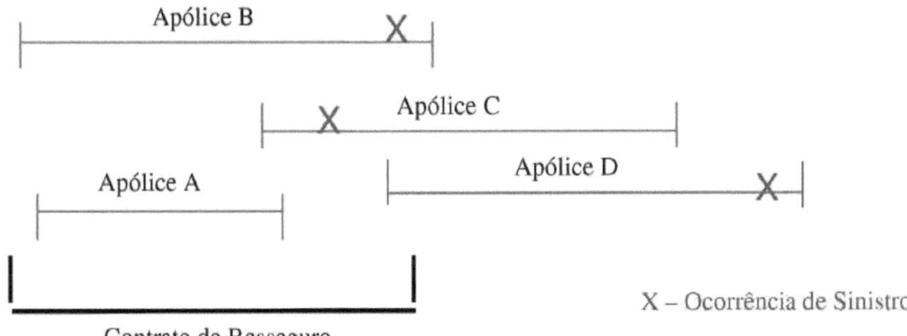

Figure 9: Example of Risk Attaching

Source: Own

3.3.4.2. Loss Occuring Basis

This criterion is based on the claim occurrence date, that is, all claims occurring within the validity period of the reinsurance contract will be guaranteed.

"Guarantees claims occurring within the contract period, even if the policies are effective before the contract." (Fontana, 2009, p.24).

The following figure exemplifies the coverage criterion for reinsurance contracts using the loss occuring criterion.

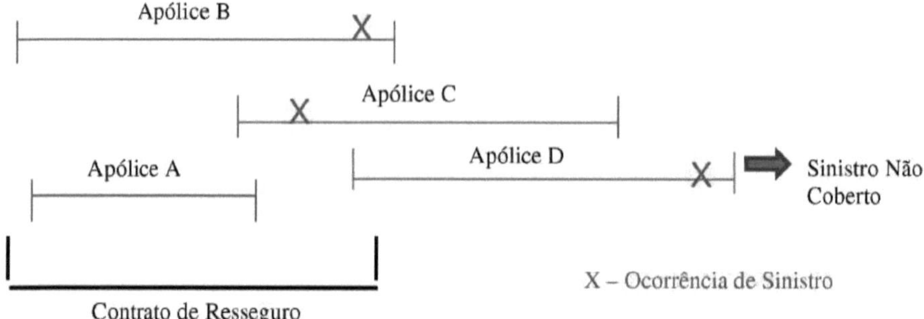

Figure 10: Example of vigency loss occuring.

Source: Own

CHAPTER 4

The Opening of the Market

4.1 Overview of the Brazilian Reinsurance Market

O reinsurance in Brazil, until 1939, was conducted almost entirely abroad, directly or via reinsurers operating in the country. From this perspective, they realized the need to create a reinsurance entity in the country in order to strengthen domestic insurers, maximizing retention and business volume, thus maintaining the premium that was passed on to other countries, within Brazil.

In this context the IRB was created by an act of President Getúlio Vargas, through Decree-Law No[5] 1.186 on April 3, 1939, in the form of a mixed economy society, with 50% of state capital and 50% of private insurance companies. The control was exercised by the Union, as holder of ordinary shares. The preferred shares, on the other hand, belonged to the private insurance companies.

Below are some very important articles of Decree-Law No.[5] 1.186:

Art. 1 The Instituto de Resseguros do Brasil (IRB) is hereby established, with legal personality and head office in the city of Rio de Janeiro.

Art. 2 - The establishment of branches or agencies of the Institute in the country and abroad is permitted.

Art. 3 - The purpose of the Institute is to regulate reinsurance in the country and to develop insurance operations in general.

Art. 20 - Insurance companies are obliged to reinsure to the Institute the liabilities exceeding their own retention for each isolated risk.

In 1966, President Castelo Branco regulated insurance and reinsurance operations through Decree-Law No.[5] 73 of November 21, 1966, providing for the National System of Private Insurance.

The following figure shows the IRB's relationship with cedants during the reinsurance market monopoly.

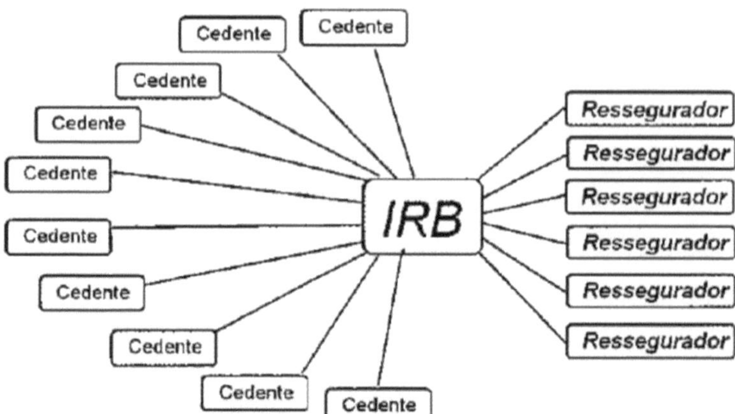

Figure 11: Relationship of the IRB before the opening of the market.

Source: Own

We can observe in the figure above that the IRB operated as the intermediary of the insurers, centralizing operations and choosing how much to pass on to the international reinsurance market.

However, the monopoly of the IRB, despite achieving its initial goal, did not follow the international reinsurance market, which annually launched modern and new products in various branches of insurance. These products were always developed for the sake of competitiveness and differentiation of reinsurers due to competition. As the IRB had a monopoly, there was no such dedication. It used as a basis for its operation, a General Standard of Reinsurance and Retrocession (N.G.R.R.) that defined the entire process of accepting risks, setting premiums and settlement of claims.

4.2. Opening of the Brazilian Reinsurance Market

On January 15, 2007, with the enactment of Complementary Law n[5] 126, new institutions were allowed to enter the national reinsurance market.

Reinsurance and retrocession operations may be carried out with the following types of reinsurer: Local, Admitted and Eventual. Below are some characteristics of each one:

Local Reinsurer

- Reinsurer headquartered in the country, in the form of a limited liability company with the exclusive purpose of carrying out reinsurance and retrocession operations;
- Minimum Capital: R$ 60.000.000,00;
- Subject to the same obligations provided for in the legislation, regulations and normative acts applicable to insurers;
- Insurers must contract with local reinsurers at least 40% of each reinsurance cession in automatic and facultative contracts in accordance with CNSP Resolution 225 of 2010.

Reinsurer Admitted

- Obliged to have a representative office in Brazil;
- Must have, bound to Susep, the minimum equivalent to R$ 5,000,000.00 to operate in all branches or US$ 1,000,000.00 to operate in the personal branch;
- Must underwrite, for more than five years, local and international reinsurance in the classes in which it intends to operate in Brazil;
- To have a solvency evaluation by a rating agency recognized by Susep;
- To have proof of permission in the country of origin for the movement of freely convertible currencies, for the fulfillment of reinsurance abroad;
- Disclose periodically balance sheet and income statement of the last fiscal year, with the respective independent auditors' reports;

Eventual Reinsurer

- Foreign company based abroad with no representative office in the country;

- Insurers may only cede to occasional reinsurers up to 10% of the total value of premiums ceded in total operations in each calendar year;
- Must underwrite, for more than five years, local and international

reinsurance in the classes in which it intends to operate in Brazil;

- To have a solvency evaluation by a rating agency recognized by Susep;
- It is forbidden for the company to have its registered office in a tax haven;
- Proof of permission in the country of origin for the movement of freely convertible currencies, for compliance with reinsurance abroad;
- Disclose periodically balance sheet and income statement of the last fiscal year, with the respective independent auditors' reports.

The IRB was authorized to exercise its reinsurance and retrocession activities, without any solution for continuity, regardless of governmental requirements and authorization, qualifying as a local reinsurer.

Today the IRB is a private limited company and mixed economy, linked to the Ministry of Finance. Its activities are concentrated in reinsurance operations in the country and abroad.

On January 15, 2007, new institutions were allowed to enter the national reinsurance market, but the market was only effectively opened on April 17, 2008, with the entry into force of CNSP Resolution n^5 168.

After the opening of the market and the end of the monopoly, the IRB and other reinsurers in the country began to be regulated by the National Council of Private Insurance (CNSP) and the Superintendence of Private Insurance (Susep).

The figure below shows how the interaction of insurers with the IRB and other reinsurers after the opening of the market became.

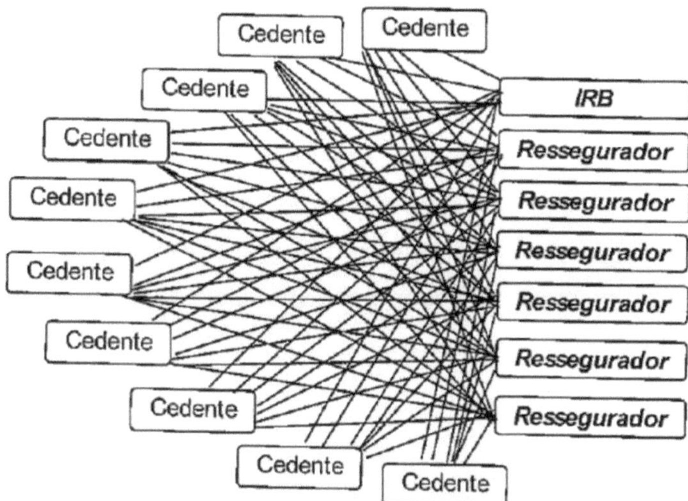

Figure 12: Relationship of the IRB after the opening of the market.

Source: Own

Currently, with the new market model, the IRB began to interact in the market with other reinsurers, needing to improve its internal controls and the level of operational efficiency as a way to mitigate possible competition disputes.

Below is a timeline of how the reinsurance market rules have been changed in order to stimulate creation and local reinsurers and competition between reinsurers.

2007/2008 - Complementary Law 126.

- Intra-group transactions must be communicated to Susep;
- Preferential offer of 60% to local reinsurers;
- In the event of non-acceptance of reinsurance cover by local reinsurers, ceding companies may carry out operations with admitted and occasional reinsurers (CNSP Resolution 164/2007);

- Local insurers and reinsurers may not cede more than 50% of the premiums written, except for guarantee insurance, export credit insurance, rural insurance and domestic credit insurance;

- Susep may authorize higher percentages provided that they are justified;
- Reinsurance transactions must be carried out with local reinsurers, admitted or occasional;
- Retrocession operations, with the same or local insurance companies;
- Reinsurance transactions concerning survivorship life insurance and complementary pension plans are exclusive to local reinsurers;
- The insurance regulator may establish limits and conditions for retrocession of risks.

2010 - Supplementary Law 137

- Funds whose sole purpose is to cover rural insurance risks in the agricultural, livestock, aquaculture and forestry sectors are deemed equivalent to local reinsurers;
- Preferential offer of 40% to local reinsurers;
- Liabilities assumed in insurance, reinsurance and retrocession may not be transferred to companies linked or belonging to the same financial conglomerate based abroad;
- Reinsurance agreements may provide for a claim control clause in favour of the local reinsurer, when it has a higher proportional share of the risk;
- A fund whose sole purpose is to cover rural insurance risks in the agricultural, livestock, aquaculture and forestry modalities is authorised to contract reinsurance.

2011 - CNSP Resolution 232 and CNSP Resolution 233

- The local insurer or reinsurer may not transfer more than 20% of the premium for each coverage to companies linked or belonging to the same financial conglomerate based abroad, except for the guarantee, export credit, rural, domestic credit and nuclear risks;
- Transfers are authorized under the terms previously mentioned, exclusively when the insufficient offer of capacity by admitted and occasional local reinsurers is proven;

- Situation of insufficient offer of capacity is defined when all local, admitted and occasional reinsurers are consulted and, as a whole, refuse, totally or partially, the risk per object of cession;
- In the event of partial acceptance of the risk, only the portion not covered may be assigned.

4.3. *The Current Reinsurance Market*

Currently, after the breaking of the state monopoly of the IRB and the opening of the Brazilian reinsurance market, most of the large reinsurers in the world are already installed in the country. This brings to Brazil new concepts of technology applied to the insurance market and new products, with coverage that was not practiced before. As the national insurance market has shown a high growth rate over the last decade, well above the GDP in the last year, it is expected that the number of reinsurers registered and authorized to work in the country will continue to grow in the coming years.

Insurers, especially the smaller ones, are being forced to become more professional since they will no longer be guaranteed reinsurance cover for all their risks, as was the case at the time of the IRB monopoly.

With the entry of many reinsurers in the country, the professional market is heated and, in a way, with a deficiency of professionals prepared and qualified for this new scenario. During the 69 years of monopoly, the training of professionals trained to face a free competition environment was not a priority.

Below is a list of the current admitted and occasional local reinsurers registered and authorised to operate in the Brazilian market.

Local Reinsurers
Ace Resseguradora S.A.
Austral Resseguradora S.A.
Alterra Resseguradora do Brasil S.A.
Chartis Resseguros Brasil S.A.
IRB-Brasil Resseguros S.A

J. Malucelli Participações em Seguros e Resseguros S.A
Mapfre Re do Brasil Companhia de Resseguros
Munich Re do Brasil Resseguradora S.A.
Swiss Re Corporate Solutions Brasil Seguros S.A
Terra Brasis Resseguros S.A
XL Resseguros Brasil S/A

Reinsurers Admitted
Arden Reinsurance Company LTD
Catlin Insurance Company (UK) LTD
Everest Reinsurance Company
Factory Mutual Insurance Company
Federal Insurance Company
General Reinsurance AG
Hannover Ruckversicherung AG
HDI-Gerling Welt Service Ag
Liberty Mutual Insurance Company
Lloyd's
Mapfre Re Companía de Reaseguros S.A.
Odyssey Reinsurance Company
Partner Reisurance Europe Public Limited Company
Royal & Sun Alliance Insurance PLC
Scor Global Life U.S. Re Insurance Company
Scor Reinsurance Company
Swiss Reinsurance America Corporation
Swiss Reinsurance Company Ltd
Tokio Marine & Nichido Fire Insurance Co. Ltd
Torus Specialty Insurance Company
Transamerica International Re (Bermuda) Ltd
Transatlantic Reinsurance Company
XL Re Latin America Ltd
Zurich Insurance Company

Eventual Reinsurers	
Arch Insurance Company	Lig Insurance Company Ltd
Aspen Insurance UK Ltd	Mapfre Empresas, Compania de Seguros y Reaseguros, S.A
Assicurazioni Generali S.p.A	Mitsui Sumitomo Insurance Company of America
Atradius Reinsurance Ltd	Munchener Ruckversicherungs-Gesellschaft Aktiengesellschaft in Munchen
Axa Corportate Solutions Assurance	National Liability & Fire Insurance Company
Axa France Vie	Navigators Insurance Company

Axis Reinsurance Company	Nouvelle Compagnie de Réassurances
Baloise Insurance Ltd	Office National Du Ducroire
Caisse Centrale de Reassurance	Paris Re America Insurance Company
CNA Insurance Company Limited	Platinum Underwriters Reinsurance, INC.
Compaigne Française D'Assurance Pour Le Commerce Extérieur	R+V Versicherung AG
Delta Lloyd Schadeverzekering N.V.	Reaseguradora Patria, S.A.B
Ecclesiastical Insurance Office Plc	Samsung Fire & Marine Insurance Co. Ltd.
Endurance Reinsurance Corporation Of America	Scor Global P&C SE
Eventual Reinsurers	
Euler Hermes American Credit Indemnity Company	Scor Switzerland Ag
Eurasia Insurance Company JSC	Seguros Inbursa, S.A.
FM Insurance Company Limited	Sirius America Insurance Company
General Insurance Corporation of India	Sirius International Insurance Corporation
Glacier Reinsurance AG.	Solen Versicherungen Ag
HCC International Insurance Company PLC	Sompo Japan Insurance Inc
HDI-Gerling Industrie Versicherung AG	Swiss Re Europe S.A
Houston Casualty Company	The New India Assurance Company Ltd
Hyundai Marine & Fire Insurance Co.	Tokio Millennium Re (UK) Limited
IF P&C Insurance Company LTD.	Travelers Casualty And Surety Company Of America
Infrassure Ltd.	W.R. Berkley Insurance (Europe) Limited
Korean Reinsurance Company	XL Insurance Company Ltd
Liberty Mutual Insurance Europe Ltd	Zurich Insurance Public Limited Company

After 69 years of monopoly, the IRB has been living for some years in an extremely competitive environment. However, currently the IRB Resseguros S.A. holds just over 60% of the market's reinsurance premiums. Despite the competitiveness the opening also brought bonuses to the IRB, since it can select the risks it wants to have in its portfolio, no longer having the obligation to accept all the risks of the country.

Below are the indicators of the numbers of local reinsurers, according to Susep's data.

January to December - 2012		
Reinsurer	**Reinsurance premium**	**Participation**
ACE REESSEGURADORA S.A.	R$218 .318.401,00	7,67%
CHARTIS RESSEGUROS BRASIL S.A.	R$28 .994.684,00	1,02%
ALTERRA REESSEGURADORA DO BRASIL S.A.	R$16 .178.553,00	0,57%
AUSTRAL REESSEGURADORA S.A.	R$ 92.313.664,00	3,24%
IRB BRASIL RESSEGUROS S.A.	R$ 1.737.831.898,00	61,06%
J. MALUCELLI RESSEGURADORA S.A.	R$ 105.115.957,00	3,69%
MAPFRE RE DO BRASIL COMPANHIA DE REESSEGUROS	R$ 195.377.112,00	6,87%
MUNICH RE DO BRASIL RESSEGURADORA S.A.	R$ 362.239.459,00	12,73%
SWISS RE BRAZIL REINSURANCE S.A.	R$ 15.376.640,00	0,54%
TERRA BRASIS RESSEGUROS S.A.	R$ 1.973.703,00	0,07%
XL REINSURANCE BRAZIL S.A.	R$ 72.247.005,00	2,54%
TOTAL	R$ 2.845.967.076,00	100,00%

CHAPTER 5

Conclusion

In the course of this work, the objective of this paper was to present the relevance of the reinsurance business, the importance of technical knowledge of reinsurance, the legislation that followed its evolution within the national scope and the main considerations about the process of opening of the Brazilian reinsurance market, with the concomitant break of the monopoly of the Instituto de Resseguros do Brasil S.A. (IRB).

Initially, it was noted that the purpose of reinsurance is to provide technical and financial stability to insurance companies, and its international nature derives from the application of the principle of mutuality between insurers and reinsurers, thus ensuring the spreading of risks.

In its history, it can be seen that reinsurance has accompanied the evolution of economic development, suffering sanctions and benefiting from relevant historical events. Meanwhile, one can see the wisdom of the implementation of the

monopoly in the country, at the time of former President Getúlio Vargas, when the performance of the IRB contributed in a very relevant way to the consolidation of the Brazilian insurance market, where, until then, was predominantly led by foreign insurance companies.

The IRB, during the 69 years of monopoly, had a key role in strengthening the national insurance companies, which were strengthened during the monopoly period. They were prepared technically and economically to face competition with foreign insurers in an open market environment.

The opening of the Brazilian reinsurance market accompanied, although somewhat belatedly, the evolution of the insurance and reinsurance market in the world, which has been developing, like the economy, over the years. With this new scenario, insurers are free to negotiate their contracts, both automatic and facultative, with the reinsurer or reinsurers that best meet their needs.

Freeing up the market allows a direct relationship between insurers and reinsurers, stimulating the launch of new and innovative products. Furthermore, the breaking of the monopoly allows free competition, enabling an eventual reduction in the insurance premiums paid by the insured and the reinsurance premiums paid by the insurer.

Although the Brazilian reinsurance market is open, the federal government, through the National Council of Private Insurance and the Superintendence of Private Insurance, has adopted the necessary measures to avoid unfair competition between insurers and reinsurers and, mainly, the export of insurance and reinsurance premiums outside the country, keeping the technical reserves of local companies invested in the country itself.

Thus, it is concluded that the break of the IRB monopoly was necessary for the evolution of the Brazilian insurance market, bringing two major advantages in the medium term: the technological advancement of local companies and the logical consequences of free competition, *i.e.,* better prices or services, benefiting insurers and, consequently, the insured.

Bibliographical References:

ABER - Brazilian Association of Reinsurance Companies. Available at: <www.aberesseguros.org.br>.

ALVIM, Pedro. National Insurance Policy - Neo Liberalism, Globalization and Mercosul. Iº Ed., São Paulo: Manuais Técnicos de Seguro, 1996.

BERNSTEIN, Peter L. Challenging the Gods: The Fascinating Story of Risk. Jonh Willy & Sons. Translation: Ivo Korytowski. 9º Ed. Rio de Janeiro: Campus, 1997.

BIDINO, Maria. Presentation of the Microinsurance and Reinsurance Market. Rio de Janeiro: CNSeg, 2009.

CHAN, Betty Lilian, SILVA, Fabiana Lopes da, MARTINS, Gilberto de Andrade, Fundamentos da Previdência Complementar: da Atuária à Contabilidade. São Paulo: Atlas, 2006.

DI GROPELLO, Giullio; MANGHETTI, Giovanni. Principles of reinsurance technique: financial reinsurance and derivatives in reinsurance. Translation by Maria Helena Bidino. Rio de Janeiro: Funenseg, 1997.

FENASEG (National Federation of Insurers). Available at <www.fenaseg.org.br>.

FUNENSEG (National Insurance School). Available at: <www.funenseg.org.br>.

. Classics of Reinsurance. Iº Ed., Rio deJaneiro: Funenseg, 2010.

. Digital Archive of FUNENSEG. Rio de Janeiro: Funenseg, 2010.

FONTANA, Nelson. Reinsurance in 8 (eight) basic lessons. Iº Ed., Rio de Janeiro: Funenseg, 2009.

GALIZA, Francisco. Economics and Insurance - an introduction. Iº Ed., Rio de Janeiro: Funenseg, 1997.

GERMAINE, John. Keep things a proportion, The Review. Cambridge: 1985.

GROSSAMANN, M. Reinsurance - an introduction, edited by the Institute of Insurance Economics of the University of St. Gallen. 3º Ed., Switzerland: 1990.

HARRISON, Connor M. Princípios e Práticas de Reesseguro. IºEd., Rio de Janeiro: Funenseg, 2007.

IRB Brasil Resseguros S.A. (Reinsurance Institute of Brazil). Available at: <www.irb.gov.br>.

MELLO, Sérgio Barroso de. The Excess of Damage Reinsurance as a useful tool against losses from environmental catastrophes and terrorist acts. April. 2205. - Available at: <www.pellon-associados.com.br>.

NASCENTES, Célio Olympio. Curso de resseguro e retrocessão. I° Ed., Rio de Janeiro: Funenseg, 1986.

FERREIRA, Paulo Pereira. Pricing and Ruin Models for Short-Term Insurance. Rio de Janeiro: Funenseg, 1- Edition - 2002, 2^ reprint - 2010.

SANTANA, Pedro. Presentation Principles of Reinsurance. Rio de Janeiro: Funenseg, 2008.

SUSEP (Superintendence of Private Insurance). Available at: <www.susep.gov.br>.

SWISS RE. Introduction to Reinsurance. I° Ed., Swiss Re, 1999.

VERGARA, Sylvia Constant. Projetos e relatórios de pesquisa em administração. São Paulo: Atlas, 2000.

Printed by Books on Demand GmbH, Norderstedt / Germany